you say. say.

Editors: Ice, Jane Ormerod

Senior Editor: Brant Lyon

you say. say.

ISBN: 978-0-9799792-1-7

Library of Congress Control Number: 2009928782

First edition

Printed in the United States of America

Uphook Press, New York

www.uphookpress.com

you say. say.

■Uphook Press■

CONTENTS

We say, say, welcome to this new anthology from Uphook Press, our next step in promoting a nationwide community of performing poets.

In considering work for publication we read the poems out loud to imagine what they might sound like on stage. From our own experience as performance poets and hosts of reading series, we've found that the poets who excite us most have these characteristics in common: distinctive voice, rhythm, risk, and reach; and that they readily transition from ink to mike and back with less of a leap than a glide. They are quick-witted, adaptable, generous—engaging both reader and listener with equal skill.

And the poets here are sensitive to the visual impact of words that sparkle on the page and in performance spark off it. Thandiwe Shiphrah and Alex O. Bleecker use spatial arrangement to convey auditory silences and fragmented speech, Shiphrah even inserting a moment of laughter in her "wild talk of multidimensionality." Compare to Michael Shorb's "Whale Walker's Morning," hooking us with his lyrical fish tale told in the tradition of the narrative.

Starbucks to whale walkers, porno to honeymooning in Michigan, Dr. Octagon, Old Rasputin—they write the gamut from cranky operettas to the ping of a microwave signaling the end.

Our poets are writing in Dagsboro (DE), Fairmont (WV), New York and San Francisco, and two Portlands—Maine and Oregon. They come from backgrounds in acting, storytelling, jazz, bongo-pounding, Def Jam slammin', truck driving, art, even opera singing.

Live poetry flourishes in small towns and large urban centers everywhere: in wine bars and dive bars, street corners and junkyards, ballrooms and cellars. Samantha Barrow even hops on her motorcycle to take her poetry on the road, reciting it wherever she is welcome (and sometimes not).

Now turn this page. Read with both eye and ear.

LAURA LeHEW

THE EFFECT OF EVIDENCE IN CONVINCING THE MIND

I am a smoky scent of discontentment
a room darkened to tongues, no
tongues, a hand on my buckle
the nervous rattle of pop bottles
displaced as we shuffle
in a three dimensional space hands
fumble each article of clothing
we caress.

I am a printing proof on the table draped
for the Operation that's going to be attempted
to remove the wrench from my thorax without setting off
any buzzers without making my nose light-up
burnt sienna in hopes of opening me—
the perfect vessel.

I am tungsten, a filament alighted by touch—
and everywhere a field of chairs.

SAMANTHA BARROW

WOULD YOU BLANK

If I took off my __________________
would you _____________________________?

If I let go of my __________________
could you ____________________________?

If I needed to _____________________
would you _____________________?

Someone told me recently I was very adjective noun.

If I took off my status
would you admire?

If I let go of my shoulders
could you silence?

If I needed it back
would you give?

Someone told me recently I was very classic butch.

If I took off my breast bone
would you hear it?

If I let go of my charm
could you stand it?

If I needed to run
would you beg?

Someone told me recently I was very special lady.

If I took off my skin
would you match it?

If I let go of my deal
could you win it?

If I needed to suckle
would you feed it?

SAMANTHA BARROW

ONE ON THE BEACH FOR A BOY WHO DIDN'T LEARN
HOW TO BE A GOOD FRIEND

The things he tended
        grew and buzzed.
The lines he drew
        danced and fell where they belonged.
The games he played threw his body into the air
        spinning circles and littering small purple flowers.

But sometimes he looked in to the sky and saw
        his loneliness instead of his power.
And sometimes he poured into his books—
        the comfort there won't ask.
And sometimes his big love shrank into a walnut.
        The space around him grew hollow and those who wanted to
        warm there
were left with a shuddering draft—
        as if moving into a new house after whomever had lived there
        before
died unhappy.

JUDITH ARCANA

THE GOD OF YOUR BODY

When you walk away from people
to the deep steep gorge
where cold streams fall into mist
over rocks among trees, you meet
a rattlesnake, a red winged hawk;
you're afraid but you take the gift:
raw glory, exaltation; you are
grateful for danger and awe.

When a fierce noon goes dark
as green midnight, wind embodies
air and the gale is a wall of rock
moving, when thunderstorms run
the horizon like wolves, a hurricane
stands like a bear in the sky and tornadoes
roar like cougars, you are thrilled,
filled with a fear of greatness.

When the land flickers like skin
on a horse, rocks like the hips of a cow
walking her pasture, when earth
quakes, breaks open between
great lakes and big river, or cracks
that long western edge by the sea,
shocked desire and molten dread
converge in the god of your body.

BLACKBIRD

I am a Blackbird, black as the day is long.
Actually I take that back that was wrong, I've got it all backwards.
I'm streaked and stained with faded yesterdays
But I refuse to take back my words.
I don't bend over backwards
To please you I'm going forwards toward
The back woods and darkness.
I am deadwood.
I am ashes.
I am a Blackbird.
Actually, I take that back that was wrong, I've got it all backwards.
I am a blackboard,
Streaked and stained with faded yesterdays.
I use only bad words, I've got it all backwards
Black as daylight, white as night,
I do bend over backwards
Into my coffin made of deadwood.
Don't you just repeat these words after me, that would be like eww,
Be like me.
I am a coffin, got tissues?
The gutter's risen in my throat and I'm coughin' up,
Spittin' out cuz I can't hold it back, I got issues.
I've been a bad boy, in a bad way,
Now I'm a bad word and a bad name
So come lets Us — I, You by that I mean We
Wipe the slate unclean.

DELETION

I am deleting my account. Goodbye cruel world. (cue the violins, cue the violence.) Either way, I know my cue for a dramatic entrance and an emotional exit. Or is that an abdominal exit wound. (cue dramatic entrance music.) Hope you don't mind if I make a quiet exit. I'm going out. The nightlife is a highlight to an otherwise quiet life. A quiet exit to a silent life. (cue emotional violence.) This is a violent knife I've got to my throat. My wife is not at home. I am not at home in my life. That's all she wrote. Now cue the violins. This communiqué comes with no strings attached. That would be too much commitment. I'm on a 2 year agreement. Which ended a year ago. Now I'm on a month 2 month, week 2 week, min 2 min living day by day and paycheck to paycheck. Minute by minute I live for your text but since I never hear from you I never live. But I don't give 2 SHuggas. IT Should be here any minute now. In the meantime everybody wants to sex me 'cuz I'm a text object. I don't object to the pretext 'cuz I'm on a 2 year agreement. I live 2 disagree and beg to differ. The inference in this instance is I am not a chooser I am a beggar so I take what I can get and hate the rest. If u don't like it just say next. Which is what I think you said, in your last text. Which I never got. (cue emotional violins, cue emotional violence.) This is my life and this is my text. I hope IT gets here soon 'cuz the paramedics can't fix this. (cue emotional violins, cue emot

THOMAS FUCALORO

18

ODE TO MY DAD'S PORNO MAGS

My first wrong insight at what a woman should be

but an insight none the less

under your bed

who knew such wisdom would lie

dictating who you were

and who i was meant to be.

A page turner.

A bible salesman.

An escaped heart

flow

pours more into an ocean of never and remove

the pressure

boils over the mountains of flessshhh-toned glistened pages
upon pages

of abstract women in reality based nude

                 these economic times

                 and my mind swells.

What will my therapist think 30 years from now when i let him know

i don't need to talk

just medication

maybe some meditation

under a bed, bare

of what a woman should be

and the flow pours more into an ocean of never

a rush, streams
     through

like a decent airline
and the female passengers

all say, "Fuck me next!"

and the invitation

becomes my heart.

That's what all the ladies want
              some hard heart

              some thought
                          less eyes

              some cranial shifts

              between the thighs

and the flow pours more into an ocean of never

and your dad's porn mags are now my heart

but what about love?

And the flow pours more into an ocean of never.

ON A BONE-DRY SLOPE

Those who listen for the sound of ash
say fire is an animal
that grows by drinking
the sap of wood and bone
and speaks in guttural continuo,

gold on yellow waves
scored over black char.

*

Embers taken by wind scribe
the intent to crown
every need for rebirth
with a given fact of darkness,

that exile pulled back overnight
through borders the moon traces.

*

Guarding hope
in white light
dilutes the magical,
coyote not heard singing
the code to unlock all gates
and drop flints up moon-lit paths,

wings stacked on a bone-dry slope.

WEATHER REPORT

Weather Report. A flute over the river. A saxophone over the waste. I feel your walk in my walk, your pulse a beam of blue air across a window's diagonal. The nonstop repetition of a synthesizer's single note. Disintegrating sheets of blood fall through the water. Flickering patterns of light translate the floating text. *I will not send you into the darkness alone.*[*] Although he did, of necessity. A blood slick just beneath her reflection ringing the glass. His weapon's "negligent discharge" opened a bright hole in his thigh. Someone boning kippers and someone dropped her knickers. Neon letters throb an emergency. Light a cigarette and it will go away. Extinguish the cigarette and only the music remains. Weather report. The atmospherics before the dance. I hear your voice in my voice, see not with but through your eyes. A massive translucent wave and inside its glassy curve a dolphin speeding its length.

*Cormac McCarthy, *The Road.*

I DON'T KNOW WHAT

The seasons have picked up speed. Snowdrifts bent the fences. Telephone poles strung out the white miles of wind. Wind blew the sunlight. The gorgeous rain. Draw an ellipse, spin it, then add a cloud of stars. Cosmic grit. Before he peed urine lyrics blood. What oats soft with moisture her pubic hair was. Also yours. Bacteria capture the earth's magnetic field. Migrate. As do we. *Do not drive at night do not take bullets guns or drugs*. We're out of flowers in English. Conscripted Latin is next. A brain atlas proposed for the mouse. Was it his fault? Was it ours? At every opportunity repeat the words: Salt marsh harvest mouse. Salt march harvest mouth. Malt harsh marvest south.

The dog with the thirst. A still life passes in a car. Always a clue. Cloud mechanics. Your face lost against the light. An apocalyptic goat plus an apoplectic owner. So sleepy he couldn't get to the end of the phrase. A word with a thousand meanings, the same meaning in each of a thousand words. Porcupines float. Wind blew her hair into the next county. More shit than you've ever been able to imagine. A corpse of a different choler. You never know what to expect of the young. *Besame besame mucho*. Kiss me a lot. You leave a lot. To be desired. And. It works. You've turned to salt again babe.

ALEX O. BLEECKER

EXPECTING

In the rawest waters   before a fish is formed   no gravity happens. This

is before born. This   is before

absence

A lack of red   on the sheets indicates

          a nascent being. Beginning   with a stain (missing)

all the universe   in a drop of blood, and then

not

                              *

When man thought to divorce God   from self   (and named him *Him*)

we all felt   the emptiness of birth

                              that loss of worth   a mother feels

the moment her child goes

                              outside

*

Releasing the names of birds   from the center   of her chest

a woman   unbuttons her shirt

                         unburdens   her breast

ROOSTER TAIL U.S.

Cocks which come from any distance are almost always favorites,
for the theory is the man would not have dared to bring it
if it was not a good cock, the more so the further he has come.
  Clifford Geertz

On our first road trip I taunt, *I've seen an awful lot.*
My imaginary cock drives and says, *You're wrong.*

We top 75, 85, and 99 on I-80, I-35, I-10, I-25
around the clock, buying soda pop at every pit stop.

In Phoenix we pet a jock's cockatiel that mocks
a smoker's cough and balks at front door knocks.

In Tucson with cockade caps cocked, we cruise
the block of cops who've caught con men.

At the Grand Canyon we spot a hawk, stalk a flock,
pocket limestone rocks, and walk a pure cocker spaniel.

We sock away cockleshells under a dock in San Diego.
In Tehachapi we're shocked by the cockcrow. We cock

bb guns and bet the stock on cockfights in Bakersfield.
After Albuquerque, White Sands, Carlsbad Cavern,

my imaginary cock and I get cockeyed in Roswell.
We sip cocktails in Colorado Springs. We're cocky

in the Garden of the Gods, cocksure atop Pikes Peak,
half-cocked in Denver with a cockney over half-pints.

We hit traffic clots in Utah, Nevada, and Washington.
We fly in the cockpit to Fort Walton Beach and Chicago.

We layover in Vermont, Arkansas, Florida, and Iowa
where we read the caucus results and cheer for our cause.

In a Texas ol' mom and pop we're shocked
by a knot of cockroaches, but order hot crock-pot chili.

Our last tourist spot is a desert plot at the zoo
where an Australian cockatoo talks and squawks.

My cock says, *Next time I'll take you places
you've never been, show you things you've never seen.*

I snort, unlock the door. My cock says, *Moloch!
The Loch Ness Monster! Cyclops! Cockatrices!*

We see and see again,

and in the waying
an immaculate sea begins to spread
rendering starch and inky tendrils through the dead
light of reckoning, till an instant
recognition forces sight into a new spree
and we connoiter in a lidless world.

Stab the eye, stab the sea, and be
another messenger of mutable delight; and when we fight
for all the bounty of our fractured sight,
let's constantly recall the limitless melee
which in the optic love, unlike the world,
we have, and have to see.

$ SANDWICH $

What to do?
The noose's loop draws tighter
Lethal needle's sting, burn of toxic gas sharper
& You've no posterity no children, spouse, indulge'd pets
Cannot ascend to paradise with mammon
What to do?
Order up two hunks of bread
Fold; insert the bill, crisp green
Say quick grace *"In God We Trust"*
Open wide. Eat the riches.

Uphook Press and Ice talk with Matthew Zapruder on his writing life.

"Clicking His Internal Mechanism"

AN INTERVIEW WITH MATTHEW ZAPRUDER

Can you talk a little about what inspires you?

I like the word inspires because it has the word "spires" in it, which first makes me laugh, because the word itself describes itself (inspires has spires in it!), and I like that language can do that. And then it makes me think of seeing a mysterious building from far off, and moving towards it, which is how it feels to me to feel inspired. A possibility of adventure, that one must be alert to, and decide to follow.

There is a book called in French *Le Grand Meaulnes*, in English *The Lost Domain*, translated by Frank Davidson for Oxford World Classics, a little pink book that if anyone ever sees it please immediately buy it and then contact me so that I can buy it from you, though you won't want to give it up. I gave my copy to someone many years ago and have been looking for it ever since, which come to think of it, is exactly what happens in the book! Anyway, it is about a boy who wanders off in search of great adventures, and in his loneliness stumbles on a world that seems to be magical and otherworldly, with princesses and castles, then loses it, then finds it again. Along the way he and the reader together experience this magical world gradually resolving itself as being actual.

It is a painful and very moving allegory for growing up, but also reminds me of how the poem must move from being a private and maybe even childish fascination with one's own imagination to being something that belongs to the world and is recognizable to it. Perhaps the poem even gets spoiled or at least dented a little in that movement outwards, and loses its innocence, but also becomes something that some of us can treasure, because it's actual, maybe like a used book or one of those old postcards that can sometimes catch your eye in an antique store, and you turn it over and see someone else's writing from their vacation or whatever, and you really want to own it but also feel a little silly buying it. But you do anyway.

When you sit down to write do you always know what you'll write about?

Usually when I sit down all I really have is the desire to make a poem, which is almost not enough, yet there I am sitting down. Sometimes I attempt to trick myself by reading a book of poems or something else and telling myself this is just reading, I don't have to try to write a poem. Practically every single time I do that I immediately want to start making my own. Sometimes I will have a title or a line that I like in mind, sometimes absolutely nothing. When I write anything, whether it's a poem or an essay or an email or even the answers to these questions, I don't know what I'm going to do: I only figure out what I think in the process of doing it. Of course then I have to go back and look at what parts of the writing are essential, and which parts are just detours or dead ends. Then in the process of doing that I think of something else, and then everything changes. This can happen a couple of times or many times, it just depends. Sometimes it will all work out perfectly the first time, but that's very rare.

How do you know when a poem is finished?

I will feel a genuine satisfying click in my internal mechanism that tells me I have come to the end of this particular line of thought. It doesn't mean that nothing more could be said; on the contrary, I think poems, if they are honest, usually end in the middle of things, because that's how every single thing in life really, truly ends.

*

Matthew Zapruder is the author of two poetry collections: *American Linden* and *The Pajamaist*, selected by Tony Hoagland as the winner of the William Carlos Williams Award. His poems, essays, and translations have appeared in many publications, including *The Boston Review, Fence, Paris Review, Alaska Quarterly Review, Open City, Harvard Review, Bomb, The New Yorker,* and *The New Republic.* He is also co-translator from Romanian, along with historian Radu Ioanid, of *Secret Weapon: Selected Late Poems of Eugen Jebeleanu.* His third full-length collection of poems, *Come On All You Ghosts,* is forthcoming from Copper Canyon in 2010. He lives in San Francisco, works as an editor for Wave Books, and teaches in the low residency MFA program at UC Riverside-Palm Desert.

MORNING POEM

Your eyes are not always brown. In
the wild of our backyard they are light
green like a sunny day reflected
in the eyes of a frog looking
at another frog. I love your love,
it feels dispensed from a metal tap
attached to a big vat gleaming
in a giant room full of shiny whispers.
I also love tasting you after a difficult
day doing nothing assiduously.
Diamond factory, sentient mischievous
metal fruit hanging from the trees
in a museum people wander into thinking
for once I am not shopping. I admire
and fear you, to me you are an abyss
I cross towards you. Just look
directly into my face you said and I felt
everything stop trying to fit. And
the marching band took a deep collective
breath and plunged back into its song.

WHALE WALKER'S MORNING

Few records survive of the whale
Walkers of the 19th Century.
Primarily American, with a scattering
Of Dutch, Greek and
African, the whale walkers
Based around the Boston-
Nantucket area
Once numbered
In the hundreds.

They counted Joseph's coat,
The Minoan seed pearl and
The harmonica of the Indo-
European virgin among their lineage.

Unlike their leaner-
Visaged brothers
Of the harpoon
They staked their eliteness
To light about the feet,
Ears tuned to a keening wind,
A finer sense of balance.

Of their concrete origins in
Sea crossings, tribal dances and
The strut of mountain axemen
Not much more is known.

Some have linked them to
Rites among the Phoenicians,
Gypsies of the Asian steppes,
To the tree at the edge of the world
In Nordic mythology, to intimates
Of migration routes and open
Country roads of earth.

Of whale walking itself
A little more is known.
Both ancient oil paintings
And early brass-tint photographs
Exist, though these provide
A dusty geometry of the total picture.

A few famous individuals—
            Nordo the Aborigine,
            Jack Clappe,
            Cave-bear Eddie
Followed the practice of having
Their first walked whale
Tattooed on their chest.

At any rate, reliable depositions
Of the time attest to the
Frequent existence of large
Whale pods which made
Hours of uninterrupted
Whale walking possible.

The necessity of timing
Whale walking sessions
To coincide with periods
Just after early feedings
Along migration routes,
Coupled with the requisite
Of near-perfect weather conditions
Led to the adoption
Of two popular
Turn-of-the-century phrases:

"It's a whale walker's morning."

"A whale walker's morning
To you and yours."

SARAH SARAI

PAULOWNIA TORMEMTOSA, BRITTLE OF BARK BUT LOVELY

With a faint chemical hint of the literary
(being Lorna Doones), my once-helium tum
has seen erosion, slides and baked-in
capitalism (with fat and sugar and wheat).

Free the wheat! Free the wheat! As pages of
my Babar books turn to dust I haunt adulthood
with no daunting presence. And take it as a sign:
buy new Babar books. Alas, no follow-through.

Free the sugar! Cows'll plod on the lawn if
dairy's freed and there'll go contemplation of
the Royal Pawlownia leafy leafy across my
bench where squirrels believe me benefactress.

Truth be I'm not contemplating, I'm allowing
botanical diversity to enter into agreement with
my innards. *Accept us*, it stipulates, *And we
shall give you one shaded moment's peace.*

Need I mention a park's powers of persuasion
at cool 8 in the green a.m.? When the Japanese
aren't improving on nature or anime they claim
this tree means hope or is used for hope chests.

In my ruffle-sole jammies, beguiled and child
enough to believe, I this time follow through.

KARIN SPITFIRE

LIBRETTO FOR MEENA: FOUNDER OF THE
REVOLUTIONARY ASSOCIATION OF AFGHANI WOMEN

I have learned to make these
scratch marks
match
the sounds
of the voices all around

I have learned to connect
one mark
to the next
to make words
of the sounds of my people all around

I have learned to piece together
the abstracted construction of table, recipe, photosynthesis
compiled into theories of relativity, divinity,
the oppression of women

I have spent hours in wondrous magic
falling into someone's imagination
finding a corner in the house to escape
or a hammock to relax, expand, travel

Because I can read
I have been to hafiz, rumi, anne frank, eli wiesel, pablo neruda
I have been to the good earth, geishaland, doris lessing
I have been to more worlds than any astronomer

solved more mysteries than scotland yard,
had more discussions in feminist theory than harvard

I have learned to
shape
these scratches, hatches, and
assemble grocery lists, kitchen table notes,
letters to editors, master thesis
I have learned to enjoy
the effort of plucking
ephemeral pre-cognizance from my belly and
turning it into verse

Somewhere between learning
these marks for the king's english
and the waxed tip scratches of pysanky,
the unbroken symbolic shamanistic tradition of my forebears,
somewhere between these schemes of
communicating meaning

the facts exist
an Afghani poet Nadia Anjuman was beaten to death by her husband
the poetry in her voice too much for him
and
when I slithered out from under the weight of my father's body and rifle
I could already read and write

Somewhere between
cave painting and universal literacy

   the facts exist
      the authentic voice of any woman
         can be sucked into a black hole
            by the fisted scripture of male hubris
    or
                  fed inflammatory morsels of raging freedom
           because some sister somewhere
        has learned to speak her truth and
    acts on it

43

THE MARTHA STORIES

Perhaps we will come to know the realized is not chronological.
  Anonymous

  1.

spent morning pondering   antecedent of memory

  2.

by afternoon no longer smitten with the Greeks or what the felled tree hears

seeking satisfactory one-sentence explanation   echo

  3.

night can't rob her of shadows remembered

conch put to mouth summons sea

hands listen like good stone

4.

what is quantifiable

she wears plum-colored scarf

has well-sculptured calves

prepares meal vibrant color   unexpected coupling

5.

perhaps   she was afraid   of chipping of nail

afraid   what she needs   lacquer can't preserve

afraid   she's too dependent upon words

afraid   when she overuses a word   it's wiped from memory

who will she be   without *word*   *& afraid*

45

FOX

Somewhere around the red fox
I plant my fibs and cranky operetta.
Within the fox pump omens
And immaculate botches,
My own forgettables, regrettables.

In the den, where the kits sniff,
I handle wet rosebud and gnawed turtle shell.
This is where the curses spark,
Where the vixen lies.

But when mornings reveal fox faces
Around each treed corner,
On those dry mornings,
My vehement hex
Rattles innocuous but bewildered.

PAUL M. L. BELANGER

INFLUENCE FUSE

Like Dr Octagon,
I want to sprout eight arms when spouting off
about brain waves and raves and ways
we can enhance them till we've had enough weekend
and stop seeking entrance to the great escape
thinking maybe we can d-dance our way
into a greater reality than we have in sanity,
but like the roots, deep down, truth is found
inside a conch shell, the eardrums
of Ella and Armstrong laid back and scatting
street corner poetics because their apartments
need to be paid for and they're thirsty
for something they ain't never seen before,

like Charlie Parker, Aesop Rock, or Amiri Baraka,
a conscience electric and eclectic, dissect it and discover
the elements, the prevalence, the relevance
of innovation, the relation of forgetfulness
to remembrance to repetition,
instances of consensual instrumental dissention,
the delusion and confusion of a generation
that can't separate fact from fiction from fad,
like Atlas couldn't tell that the atmosphere
didn't merge with the ocean
when he shrugged off the parasites
with the appetites of Jack Kerouac
for new vistas and Bunyan for flapjacks
and Burroughs for a fix

so that like all hep cats they never get
fat, taxed, or lax 'cause too fast for that
they form the slim history between
you and me impregnating each other like
circular sea worms swirling in the jakes
where Sage Francis is cleaning and thinking
about the smell of urine and slime of the shit
that we're in. So praying to his lady,
say liberty what you think? Maybe we break now,
or maybe we break down

like Deltron with his space ship and lasers at his hips,
carrying out his master's orders on the moon
living just doing what he do
because we're all Jim Crow now
and these poems are gospel
as long as Whitman knows a dollar
isn't worth a soldier's life
and Hughes that dreams explode
there's hope that doing what we do,
standing on each others shoulders,
growing louder and louder
we might light the fuse,

and I want to be there.

JOAN PAYNE KINCAID

LIKE LAMBS   II

Half the day spent dealing email call
to fall or leap endlessly wilting like fallen lettuce
or empty oyster sauce
or spent orgasms in need of names to send whoever may be laughing;
of the planet and it's so hot today you fell dizzy and couldn't zip
things requiring physical effort were all left unplanned in a tizzy
pending September hurricane frazzle up on the a/c on…
rims hot as burned fried eggs;
another cycle challenge to use precious time and bring them on;
an English horn stamps a piece by Berlioz so lean
so loud and the harp a lonely blues sound in a moody bistro
a dune party when the moon was partly out stumbling on the Sound
purifying those who already wander aimlessly on
like little white clouds,
why do we all love little white clouds and clams
not to mention oysters which has already been done.

o let's exclude science and organs to leap and dance our downfall
tell please give a clue of plie-ing lambs or laughs;
women and girls go backward sip with a partner
part of it would be a portal of enter exit strategy.
no problem on textures or engaging poses.

environmental probe whoa or go
an ironic drum rollllll rim-shot!
tell the same over again…
let the names rumble tender overtures

they accept as truth raw images
and tensions at war in a guilty game;
pretend we still are safe as a non-entity…
let's pretend an affair surrounded by water

we tell ourselves to proceed under rare rounded boundaries
flavored with drops of curare but not enough to kill;
let's continue such philosophical portals
join sophistry typical of lofty medieval sophomores
let's sit and draw nude figures pretending to feel.

SUZANNE HEAGY

Pathetically coERcive

I've lost my raincoat again.
One second of every ten
red lights flash in expired parking meters.

Duck off the street and up the stairs.
The music playing underneath
is never Joni Mitchell.

Shouts hold down the floor.
If only the man at the bar drinking gin
had on a better homburg.

I won't nurse my pint.
Blind fish swim in underground rivers
even in flood lights.

I imagine you here, twisted lips
with your grin cleft-born and sewn
by excellent surgeons.

The nostril is off. It's not that I care;
it's what the door
would say about the moldings.

If you were here
I wouldn't even mention
your birth defect.

51

STAPLING THE BACKYARD TOGETHER

I sit in my gazebo in the headquarters of the freeway, hearing all the long haul trucks. Because of their exhaust, a traffic helicopter flies over and over, never meeting the flying lesson that circles beneath kite tails of higher vapor. My albatross storms out the back door, his enormous basketball body exposed in miniature shorts, and takes to the sidewalk. Lavinia Dickinson shouts from the kitchen to ask if the pollution index is too high to bake bread. A crow the size of a piece of an oil slick swoops down. Across the street, a man tries to apologize to a woman who shouts every third word. The crow drops another empty nest.

If anyone were listening, they'd hear me complaining. I say in a dispassionate voice, "If it's not chopping firewood, it's Asian beetles. There are emergencies and there are *Ee murr jen cees*. When people don't hear the sirens, a lawn chair has collapsed. Nobody can stop the lava. I regret macular degeneration, and send best wishes. Too bad for your bikini because ear wax is not water soluble."

Whoever will be strolling down the street at night will be a stranger walking a dog appropriately with a leash and plastic bag. Whoever flies over in that jet will be someone going to see their mother. Whoever is carrying a baseball bat will only smash a car window to steal a stereo. The huge bat flying circles around the environmentally offensive street lamp must be hungry. They make these wooden frogs that sound like trees. Carbon monoxide turns orange in moonlight. Two rabbits fuck in the hedges where no one can see them.

AIMEE HERMAN

52

RUMMAGING THROUGH DUMPSTERS FOR INSPIRATION

Writing is like carrying a fetus.
  Edna O'Brien

come out through   spread blood knee heritage
plasma of syntax

pre-developed demeanor
of   *o*
urged toward dash

—

airway traffic controller dialogues with weather vanes and windshield pressure
hybrid of resonance and chewing capacity

writing is like
scribbling around chalk outline of
discharge.

a monthly modulation gathering

          nothing   rhymes   with   fetus

salivary eraser exchanges   claimed
for
un

what is food for thighs rest?

slide aluminum into skull of   root word
using mortar and
hammer
                    e   a   t

scribe de-clawing testicles of
latin origin
antibacterial degreaser of
intellect

[nothing 's original when words become
faces or
snowflake fingerprints

uniqueness derives from in:
ability to   see all.

trace length of umbilical chord chase
ing
in-
creased thought-flow-speed

companion to wax
announcement where bees fly

overheard:
Q: where do babies come from?

A: cigarette boxes and microwaves

inhalation of spirits
copulating with general surgeon and
electric powered defroster

INSTRUCTIONS:
1. press high
2. cook three hours
3. defrost only when teeth give out

inhale once lungs complete lap
race of
bone structure

force may be used when   canal   refusal   exhibits   tearing

4. when measuring distance of wax paper for baking or
     breathing,
        check for durability and commitment

burns are created when bones forget to bother.

Note: You can measure the length of a small town by amount of
babies in dumpsters
*extra points received by those who stick around for interviews

everyone
deserves

their
fifteen
minutes of
]

THOMAS GIBNEY

56

OLD RASPUTIN FROM TENNESSEE

I don't deserve a feast like this
I don't deserve even a penny to my name;
who are you with your fanciful gobbledygook
and your restless earth that's worn to the bone?
O Flooooorida, Flooooorida!
I scratch and scowl like Jess's palm trees.
In Florida there's all kinds of hippies.
Rico, they make you filthy rico, a poet like me—
I've struck some reaaal gold, here.
Some real Texas tea. (Appended: *Florida Volk*—as in the
German.)
Freewheelers, don't ever change your ways!
You give us old sorcerers
all the bread we charm into stones.

57

CALLIGRAPHY

I will dig into the earth
and find the words she wrote
on yellowed paper, mailed
to her brother who served
with the Union Army near
Antietam. He received the
letter on September 13, 1862,
a bullet was mailed to him
on September 17, 1862.

The earth received him and
the letter enclosed in his
shroud, an old feed sack.
They ran out of sheets,
which were needed to dress
the wounded whose bullets
mailed them to the camp hospital.

Ink was her first word.
We are short on ink.
Since the war mother taught
me how to make this ink
with fermented berries
and burnt charcoal; it will
do for now until you return
with a new bottle.

September 25, 1862
This ink is weak; it does not
hold well, my pen is dry.
We received this notice
yesterday, a list of the
Union dead. Are your bones
with the dead or do they
stagger about trying to hold up?

Tell me you are yet
with the living.
I keep writing just in case
there is a resurrection
or an error in the count.

An·tie·tam: A creek of north-central Maryland emptying into the Potomac River. The bloody and inconclusive Civil War Battle of Antietam was fought along its banks on September 17, 1862.

59

BORDER THEORY

This afternoon smells of Michigan
the city of Petoskey
          where my parents honeymooned
thirty-nine years ago
and Antonia's sweet bread rising
in the wood oven.

Lake water
          beneath my skin
wet sand and the scent
of Northern Peninsula fish
bind me to home.

I want to fit
Michigan comfortably into Pittsburgh
but the flat, symmetrical towns
          diagonal bend of home
will not allow it.

ROBERT HARRIS

READING DANTE

1

Whole walls destroyed, a wreck,
though in a moment we're carried
into the garden, where a woman watches
pale as the moon's arc, then to a glass house
emanating darkness, suddenly lit by faces
from within, then the word *Fin*
etched on a curlicued page.

2

It's the getting there: the suck and gasp
leaking from somebody's headphones,
the lady applying eye paint and popping her gum.
Rini says *They're not like us down there.*

Tonight the dying AC adds aroma
to all the sensual contention,
and a mariachi trio in yellow and black
performs all the way across the river.

Look up! There's a snippet from Uncle Walt
at his most urgent: *Stranger! If in passing*
you would speak to me, why should you not?
And why should I not speak to you?

3

Family and murder (nothing more to be said)
a pink-tinged contract framed in paper towels
hastily hidden in an unmade bed

A witness crouches behind the drapes
trying not to see how money swirls
down a gory sink, how murder propagates

How the mind floods with vivid recall
delicate orifice against the knife
and experience turns the naïf fearful

4

All those who loved me
All I loved
All of us young again
The very and only summer
High carved ceilings lemon and white
Everyone floating from room to room
Innocent communion
No one leaving
No one lost

5

I'm New York City's boyfriend,
starting from when my aunt
was sleeping with my mom,
nights when the man
of the house went out
—most nights, until the one
that slammed it all apart.
Can I stay?

6

Earth and air
invert, purging
this one existence,
this body's throes.

MARY McLAUGHLIN SLECHTA

CHATTER

To begin with, Tariq Aziz tagged along
to Egyptian Night at the campus. That might
raise red flags, but technically was not a date.

I know. You ate at his cousin's house.
He spit olive pits in his palm and shoveled tahini
like a normal guy. He was handsome, macho.

Nothing like the seminary student you almost
danced with at the Crystal Ballroom.
He turned out fine for the country,

but you would've died of shame,
your brothers gladly belted the cheek he'd turn
after they socked the first.

I remind you about the night before the war began.
The anchors sounded regretful, as if Tariq
was somebody they too had known in a casual way.

"Splendid fellow," you could hear them thinking,
like they'd shared a pitcher the night before.
Major networks too. Not BBC for Americans.

The click-clack of knitting needles,
as we cradle our phones,
increases the overall chatter in this country.

Lately our joke about elevated alert levels
has gotten stale, so you shout your name and address
and I tell you about the urinalysis I took

after signing a waiver at the hospital
allowing access to the feds: Remember we wondered
why Reagan's polyps were displayed at dinnertime?

Well, it goes both ways. As we speak, the President
is handing my lab results to his wife,
and she's disturbed by the cloudy sample.

You're a stitch, you say.
And I say you're a stitch too.
We're two stitches that never get dropped.

And now an update about your cat:
last night he caught a mouse
and left it hypnotized on the kitchen floor.

Do I suppose he tried to drown it first?
I know, I know. How else explain the shit
at the bottom of the bowl?

And all that splashed water.
Strange, I admit.
No stranger, you say,

than the patriotic sacrifice of rubber
and ladies panties falling down
in the Second World War.

Afterwards, uniforms abandoned
on southern highways,
spit-polished boots emptied

like an alien abduction.
And those children dying,
in Vietnam, Birmingham. For what?

I know. I know.
The same age as you
and that "almost" boyfriend.

Do you ever wonder, how a tilt
of your chin and a flutter might
have spared him that awful death?

Why bother? It wasn't just the brothers,
you tell me. Every girl in the powder room
had a crystal ball:

hands too fine for fieldwork
and a mouthful of syllables,
too many for dancing slow.

THANDIWE SHIPHRAH

I LET MYSELF GO
(Some Wild Talk about Multidimensionality)

In the realm of jazz, opening my inner ears,
I hear myself calling me.

(While splayed on my old cross, there are times I wonder
Whether this me is really real).

    Contraction.

Breathing, I let the feeling of going up,
Of being joined by a horn
With a hum the color of echo echo

      "Pucker up, my friend. You've got a big kiss coming."

Circles are flirting with rectangles,
Rectangles communing with triangles,
Seed atoms collaborating like crazy (but they're not).
Laughter, like this: **HA**-ha-ha-ha-ha-ha-ha-**HA**

Who called the parade?
Why this silver and blue light display?

      "The egg cracked when it cracked."

Understand that to mean that this gathering is and is not random.

"After the breakup, a crowning split, and then the marriage *happens*,
if I can use that metaphor."

"Let **H** stand for unidentified source."

"Let **A** be indicative of desire."

Ain't nobody else here is how I heard it.

"*Ain't nobody else here* is how I heard it,
which could mean that this I am is into ease."

Nine Unseen well versed in unison:

"One, you are hiding in utero.
And here again, you are 10 years old."

"To be a hundred and one once more"

"To be a hope that was hidden and growing feathers!"

"Now this 49-year-old can finally reveal the secret she's held for 37 years."

"Look who's stepping out, feathers about to fly!"

"Who was it who said it?"

"Every birth is a matrix of organized effort."

"Am I quoting Miles or Monk?"

My last struggle was AB or AC.   I let go of B.   Now A has a
whole-different tone to it.

Beginning again?

Keep in mind that this poem might be something out of Picasso's
gymnastic imagination.

We're all part of the tension of differentiation, but who knows why?

I'm still-walking with two questions – where else? as what? – and with
no need for
What we used to call hysteria.

Another one has taken that word back, redefined it as being re-refined.

Call it a movement to sustain our own movement.

Makes good sense to me.

I mean why stop to notate if?

JOAN PAYNE KINCAID

it was the whitecaps crashing- in iii

near the car,   you were thin
and wore a petite hat

and too tight   itchy sweater   pitching a tent
in night air

down at the low tide line   he sat reading the paper
while you walked

to the town hall wall   to tell them
how like paradise they appear so high

and promise yourself   to write them
the way they watch

one after another   they watch one another
like a marathon runner

watches in front   a situation
forcing need to kick-ass…

a fight for attention   to find the key
o defeat

trying not to hiccup   after licking a forkful
of cavatelli;

Ruddy duck and gull   float up and down
in water's determined drive

to shore   before the tide turns
to ice…

(out in the morning cold   across a white sky
a crow caws warning),

as if snorkeling,   as if they were in this house
or sitting in the car

thinking thin toward night   trying to accomplish
countless things

before preparing   to write   in some form
of relationship

after the relatives   leave…

transformation from relatively calm harbor
the way things change

like dogwood   and the half dead maple
return from sleep;

what made you think   Tiddleywinks
at her home?

You don't play anymore   and she left without notice
obviously no longer at her home;

that she and you   will never be again
or do those childish button-y tricks…

sad, but really   no great loss,
after-all;

there's still coffee   on the front porch
a few peaceful moments Saturday mornings

remembering Mother's singing,   the yin yang
of it;

we respond to circumstance…the music of it…
comedy   old clothes   special events   boredom;

wind,   snow, rain, sun- melting glitter,
swish of whitecaps.

KIT KENNEDY

LAST NIGHT AT TWILIGHT A GANG-BEATING SWARMED
AROUND ME INTERRUPTING RUSH-HOUR TRAFFIC WHICH
WAS PISSED ABOUT BEING INCONVENIENCED. THIS
AFTERNOON I AM EATING A FINE LATE LUNCH AND
OVERHEARING A CONVERSATION. LATER IT RAINED.

crisp red pepper

        snap/belt
        welt on check
        crack/stick

        who sees broken ribs he feels
        against traffic
        clumsy ballet: no admission
        charge

     measuring age/wealth
     to dad across table she's talking
     24/he's 83 details
     the world takes in
     by eavesdropping

     hard-ball
     real-estate

                              her elbows poised
                              under weight
                              black silk
                              creases
                              triangle firm
                              as lips
                              until ash

note to self:
use Japanese eggplant
light touch
bean sauce
look up
properties
basil

                              she talks about dad's
                              contemporaries
                              losing
                              threads

I say
who can hear
a good story
too many times

flip a coin
umbrella
or not

zigzag
traffic
.

oh
full
belly

under cheek
welt
bleeding
descent
underground
slowly
comes
siren

SUN SONNET

A naked tree can tell us everything:
chained to the earth, grappling with sky,
we flaunt our imperfections in the rain
as budding eyes. Craven and verklempt,
it's all we can to writhe, stolidly, fatefully
arching vesicles toward luscious liquid,
saturated air, toward instant light.
And in the wind, twisting, clattering arms,
we find the flexibility of heart
to wind us for the true imbroglio,
the quickening. Oh yes, you know you know:
what roots you have, not disparate, reclaim
the mortal trunk we have and have again,
pulled upward, out, beyond our living ken.

JOANNA VALENTE

WHAT WE DON'T KNOW

bicycles lean against mustard-colored walls
in pairs like swans with handlebar necks greasy
        with tornadoed fingerprints;
a complexity Catholic school boys do not care to understand
with the same fondness as fast, kicking cars

where love stays hidden in the backseat, among
the gray lining as they cradle their sex in hands veiled
        insincere with mapped pleasures
traveling faster than legs steering bicycles, than feet driving cars
curfew at eleven, long after the orange light moves down

        toward things no one has seen.

BANG

Accelerant in a jar, exploded in cells
of a multiple bright, like the youth
I came in with, enflamed with himself

and the rest of everything he reflects—
name it or not (never said we weren't
pyromaniac). Never the stars, but a series

of sparks—drunks yelling in the street
in place of a choir, empties piled up
in the cellar of the house—all

stupefied by flame, how it becomes
a glassy contortion in the dark. Now
the altos are yelling, too, calling

their men. They move on, leaving us
to pull fire over ourselves.

CHUCK

He's particular about his particulars.
Chuck. Double mocha. Extra shot. Extra chocolate.
No whip. Not too hot if you don't mind.
He is beyond a regular. He is a moving fixture,
like the pile of ravaged newspapers on top of the trash can;
a shifting constant. The slight shake of his hand,
the tremble of his leg.
The rattle of his pills in their bottles. A phalanx
of Russian tea dolls.
Each bottle looks just big enough to contain
the one to it's left.
If it were ever empty. I've never seen them empty.
Lined up between him and the fancy glass mug
in which I serve him his coffee.
He's tearing 12 sugar packets into 48 perfect squares.
He always sits outside in the patio chair.
We don't mind the mess.
When I go out to smoke he lends me his lighter.
The safety cap has been bitten off.
A smoking chain of Camel 100 Lights in a crescent
around his right foot.
Says he misses the drugs sometimes.
        (Not like these. Like drug drugs.)
The Valium he takes now would pack a buzz
if they weren't taking the edge off the stomach pain
from the Lithium.
And then there's a dirty dozen of others

whose names I can't remember or pronounce.
They were only going to let him out of rehab
if he made a three page single-space list of all
the reasons he had to stay clean.
He said his little sister.
Not wanting his Mother to bury him.
He'd save money.
He was halfway down the second
when the seizures started.
Then they moved him to a halfway house.
Then he started hanging out here.
He can't handle a job. But he gets disability.
It's enough to live if you keep your life small.
Chuck bends the stir straws at every quarter inch. They coil
in front of the coffee. Which is in front of the pill bottles.
Which are next to the ant trail of cigarette butts.
In the center is Chuck; arms folded and legs twitching.
Chuck asks me if I ever made a fort when I was a kid.
Not like in a back yard with scrap wood. Like in your room
with couch cushions and blankets.
I say yeah. Give him back his lighter.

GARY HANNA

80

ROADSIDE

I saw a kitten
all curled up
on the side of the road,
the last thing
it knew how to do,
to be happy

CONTRIBUTORS

JUDITH ARCANA writes poems, stories, essays and books. Her most recent poetry publication is the chapbook *4th Period English* (Ash Creek Press, 2009), which explores immigration. Her other books include the poetry collection *What if your mother* (Chicory Blue Press, 2005) and *Grace Paley's Life Stories: A Literary Biography* (University of Illinois, 1993). Judith grew up in the Great Lakes region and now lives in the Pacific Northwest.

SAMANTHA BARROW rides her motorcycle around the U.S. putting poetry where it doesn't belong. She has received numerous grants for her gently erotic poetry workshops for survivors of sexual abuse. She is the author of *GRIT and tender membrane* (Plan B Press), *Jelly* (Tiger / Monkey Alliance), and her self published *Chap*. Her poetry and non-fiction have been widely published in *Off Our Backs*, *The Philadelphia Inquirer*, *The Philadelphia City Paper*, and *Lesbian Nation*. She lives in New York City.

PAUL BELANGER is a world traveler, teacher, storyteller, and poet who has performed his work in countries as diverse as South Korea and the UK. He believes in the ability of poetry to engage people in socio-political debates and to take greater responsibility in their communities. He received his degree in English from the University of Wisconsin-Green Bay and an MA in the Teaching and Practice of Creative Writing from Cardiff University, Wales.

ALEX O. BLEECKER is a teacher and poet living in Harlem. His chapbook *Found in a Cord* was published in 2006 by Poets Wear Prada Press and his work also appears in various print and online journals, including *The Squaw Valley Review, fre • quen • cy, Matter, Shampoo*, and *CLWN WR*. He has performed on radio for Columbia University's *Art Waves*. Alex is currently working with Tibetans-in-exile in Dharamsala, India.

TONY BURFIELD lives in Boulder, Colorado, and works at the public library. When not running wild in the hills, he writes, pounds on his bongos, and edits an online poetry review.

PATRICK CAHILL received a doctorate in History of Consciousness at UC Santa Cruz. While there he completed *Whitman's Photographic Eye: Vision in Walt Whitman's America*, a chapter of which appeared in *The Daguerreian Annual*. He has published fiction and poetry in *TriQuarterly*, *Reed Magazine*, *North Beach Beat*, and *North Coast Literary Review*, and recently co-produced "Celebrating 20th Century World Poetry" at SF Mechanics' Institute. Patrick and a fellow San Franciscan are launching a literary and arts review, *Ambush*, in the fall of 2009.

MALAIKA FAVORITE is a visual artist, writer, and winner of the 2005 Louisiana Literature Prize for Poetry. Her collection of poetry, *Illuminated Manuscript*, was published by the New Orleans Poetry Journal Press and her work appears also in anthologies and journals including *The Maple Leaf Rag*, *Pen International*, *Uncommon Place*, *Hurricane Blues*, *Visions International*, and *Xavier Review*. Malaika's art work can be found in collections throughout the United States. She lives in Augusta, Georgia.

THOMAS FUCALORO was born in Brooklyn, grew up on Staten Island, and now resides in Harlem. He is manager of a clothing store so he can pay for his poetry habit. Thomas says, "This is what I want to do with my life. Mom and Dad are not happy."

CHRISTIAN GEORGESCU was born in Bucharest, Romania, and raised in New York City where he has appeared on stage and in film, most recently in "Pussyfoot," which screened at the Anthology Film Archives. He has read his poetry in a variety of venues throughout New York City.

THOMAS GIBNEY reads, writes, eats, sleeps, breathes, dreams, loves, doubts, regrets, smiles, listens, waits, decants, invokes, belies, combusts. He lives in New York City by way of Tennessee and Florida.

GARY HANNA has received fellowships in poetry from the Delaware Division of the Arts and the Virginia Center for the Creative Arts. He won the Brodie Herndon Memorial Prize in 2002 and the Wallace W. Winchell Poetry Contest in 2005. His poems appear widely in literary journals and anthologies.

ROBERT HARRIS is a long-time participant in the Patricia Carlin poetry group at the New School in New York City. His poems have been published in journals including *Barrow Street*, *Crested Myna Press*, and *Spillway*.

SUZANNE HEAGY writes and teaches in northern West Virginia. Her work has appeared in *Dos Passos Review*, *Oregon Review*, *Lynx Eye*, and *Poetry Southeast*. Her novel, *Meridian Inn*, was named a finalist in the 2008 Sol Books Prose Selection Series. Suzanne is fiction editor at *Kestrel*, the literary journal of Fairmont State University.

AIMEE HERMAN spends her time counting rats in subway stations, searching for the significance of push-up bras and girdles, and disemboweling the meaning of sexuality. She currently works as a contributing writer for *Spectrum Culture* and *Weird Sisters West* and is also a managing editor of erotica for *Oysters & Chocolate*. Based in Boulder, Colorado, Aimee enjoys a severe fondness for peanut butter, individuals with curly hair, and Canadians.

KIT KENNEDY has been published widely in print and online journals including *Bombay Gin*, *Rainbow Curve*, *Saranac Review*, *FRiGG*, *Mannequin Envy*, and *Niederngasse*. She hosts the monthly Gallery Café reading series in San Francisco.

JOAN PAYNE KINCAID has published ten books of poetry and is a painter, mom, avid birder, gardener, and former opera-concert artist, living in Sea Cliff, Long Island, with her cats and dogs. Her book, *Blue Eyes Wise and Dancing*, co-authored with Wayne Hogan, is forthcoming.

LAURA LeHEW is an award-winning poet whose work has appeared in such anthologies and journals as *Eating Her Wedding Dress: A Collection of Clothing Poems* (Ragged Sky Press, 2009), *A Cappella Zoo*, *J Journal*, *Pank*, and *Untamed Ink*. Her chapbook *Beauty* came out in 2009 from Tiger's Eye Press. In addition to being a crazy cat lady living in Eugene, Oregon, Laura is busy spinning up a new publishing press named Uttered Chaos.

RICHARD LORANGER is a writer, performer, and visual artist currently residing in San Francisco. He is the author of *Poems for Teeth* (We Press, 2005), which Bob Holman called "one of the most extraordinary and virtuosic poetic feats since Francis Ponge took on Soap." Recent work can be found in *Correspondence* and *CLWN WR*. He has lived all over the darn place, and may be living in your town soon.

G. L. PETTIGREW is an educator, writer, photographer, and naturalist living in South Florida. His poetry and essays have appeared in numerous print and online publications including *Red River Review*, *Taj Mahal Review*, *Indian Country Today*, *Terrain.org*, and *Red Ink*. He served as a Cultural Consultant / Sponsor on the short independent film "The Elements of Ice."

SARAH SARAI'S poems appear in *The Mississippi Review*, *Fogged Clarity*, *The Minnesota Review*, *Ghoti*, *BigCityLit*, and other journals. Her first collection, *The Future is Happy*, is published in 2009 by BlazeVOX Press. She lives in New York City.

THANDIWE SHIPHRAH is a poet and performance artist living in Nashville. She co-produced the spoken word CD, *The Secret Marvelous Instead,* and authored two books, *Leftover Light: Poems* and *Don't Make No Sense: A Creative Response to Your Life's True Calling.* Since 1999, she has collaborated with her husband, musician / composer Daniel Arite, in the jazz-blues-folk-etc. performance duo, The Bosch Institute, presenting their "audio-collages" at the Nashville Folk Festival, the Improv Festival, Philadelphia Fringe Festival, and many other poetry / music venues.

MICHAEL SHORB'S work reflects an abiding interest in myth, history, and the lyrical form, as well as a satirical focus on present day trends and events. His poems have appeared in over one hundred magazines and anthologies including *Rattle, Poetry Salzburg Review, Michigan Quarterly Review, Commonweal,* and *Names In A Jar: 100 American Poets* (Hood Press, 2007). Michael lives in San Francisco.

MARY McLAUGHLIN SLECHTA has published a collection of poems about grief, *Wreckage on a Watery Moon* (Foothills, 2005), and two chapbooks, including a very cool illustrated collection from Feral Press. An associate editor for The Comstock Review, she resides in Syracuse, New York.

KARIN SPITFIRE is a former Poet Laureate of Belfast, Maine. Her performance poems include "Incest: It's All Relative," "Corpus Callosum," "Can I Get You Another Cocktale," and "Sports & Art." Karin's first poetry collection, *Standing with Trees,* was published in 2005 by Illuminated Sea Press.

CHARLES F. THIELMAN is a poet, artiste and the vice-president of an independent bookstore's collective in Eugene, Oregon. Born and raised in Charleston, South Carolina, he has worked as a corrections counselor, Chicago truck driver, city bus driver, shoe salesman, and Left Coast Sand-Castler. "Nowadays, my driving ambition is to be the best damn Grandfather on the planet for four — yes, four — Rascals!"

GEOFFREY JASON KAGAN TRENCHARD has performed poetry on HBO's Def Poetry Jam, at universities throughout the United States, and in numerous detention facilities. He is a mentor for Urban Word NYC and teaches a regular workshop in the foster care center at Bellevue. *The National Poetry Slam Anthology, Kitchen Sink Magazine, GetUnderground.com, Tea Party Magazine,* and *The Worcester Review* have all published his poems and essays. A member of the performance poetry troupe, The Suicide Kings, Geoffrey lives with his wife in Brooklyn.

JOANNA VALENTE lives in Yonkers, New York. She enjoys ginger tea and listening to Billie Holiday. Currently Joanna is completing her bachelor's degree in Creative Writing and Literature from SUNY Purchase College.

STEFANIE WIELKOPOLAN is a native of Michigan who dreams of having her own show dedicated to sarcasm on NPR. Her essay, "The Cultivation and Liberation of Julia Alvarez's Literary Voice," was recently published in *Confluence: The Journal of Graduate Liberal Studies* and her poems have appeared in *Zaum Press, Coe Review, Temenos,* and *Miranda Magazine.* She is a writer-in-residence for two elementary schools in Detroit and also teaches English at Henry Ford Community College in Dearborn.

LAURA MADELINE WISEMAN teaches English at the University of Nebraska-Lincoln. Her poetry and prose have appeared in *Margie, American Short Fiction, Blackbird,* plus the anthologies *Eating Her Wedding Dress* (Ragged Sky Press, 2009) and *My Little Red Book* (Twelve, 2009). Laura's chapbook, *My Imaginary,* is forthcoming from Dancing Girl Press.

■ **Uphook Press** ■

For further information, reading schedules, and submission details, please visit:

www.uphookpress.com